THE BEST OF
ARRANGED FOR GUITAR

T0041176

Arranged by Marcel Robinson

ISBN 0-634-03024-8

HAL•LEONARD®
CORPORATION

7777 W. BLUEMOUND RD. P.O. BOX 13819 MILWAUKEE, WI 53213

Visit Hal Leonard Online at
www.halleonard.com

www.yanni.com

THE BEST OF YANNI
ARRANGED FOR GUITAR

CONTENTS

Adagio in C Minor

Composed by Yanni

Slowly

*Original Key Cm.
Arranged in Em for guitar playability.

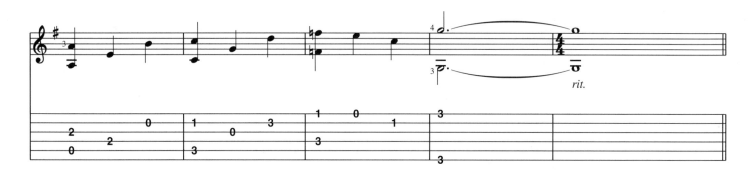

Steadily

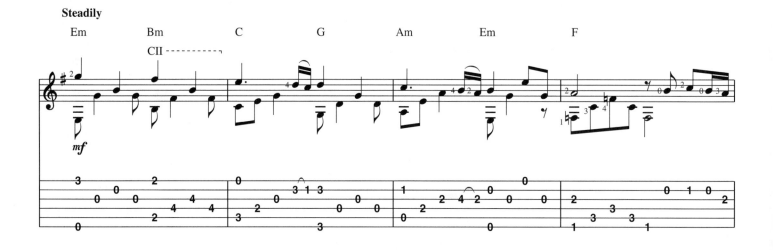

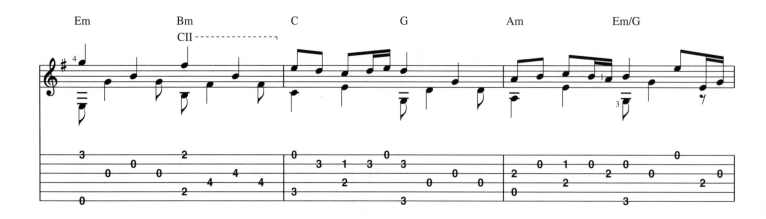

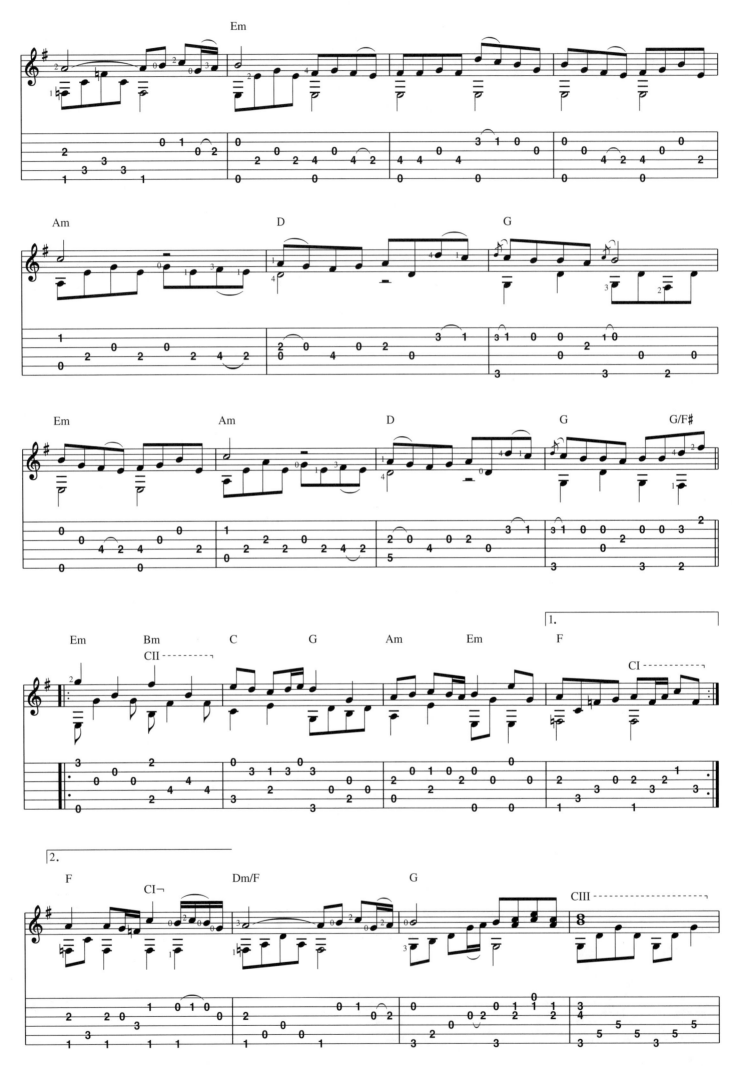

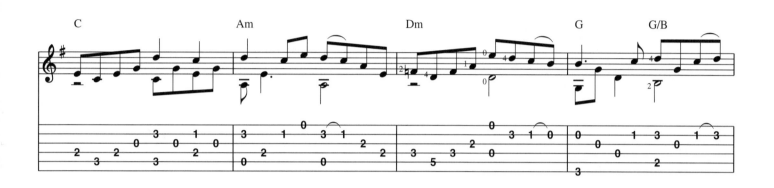

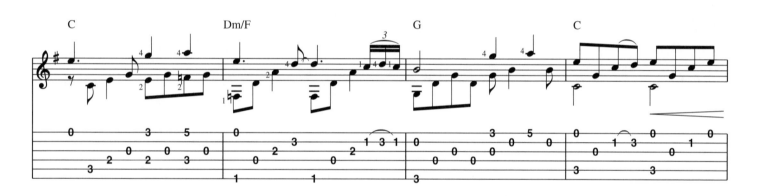

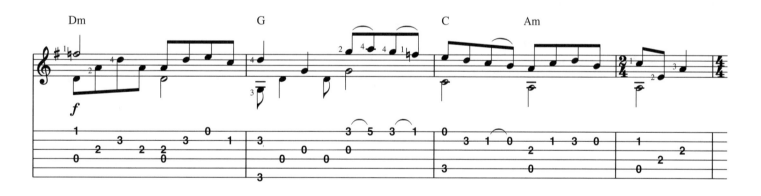

Almost a Whisper

Composed by Yanni

Slightly distant

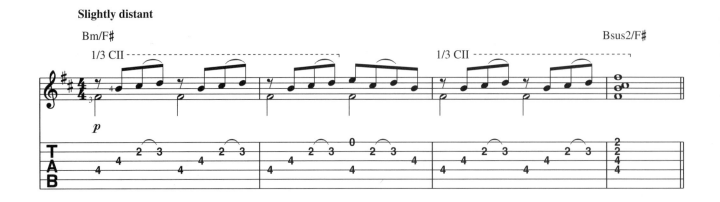

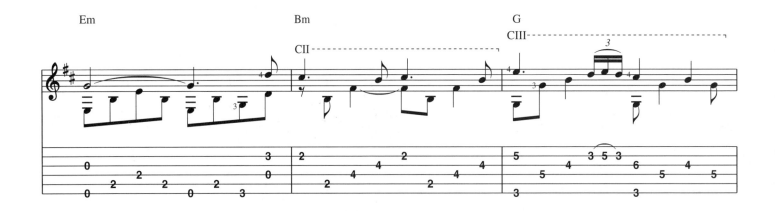

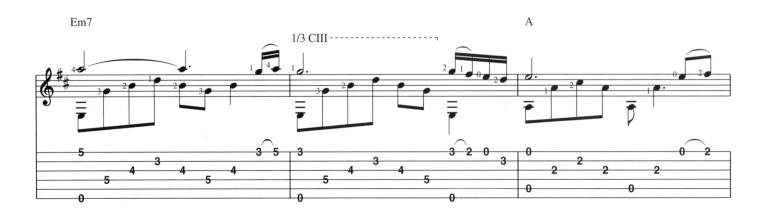

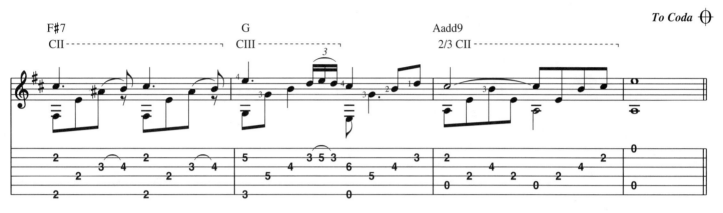

To Coda ⊕

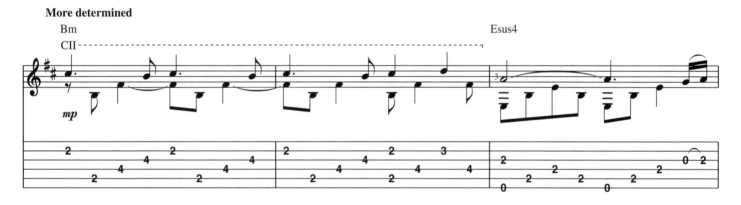

More determined

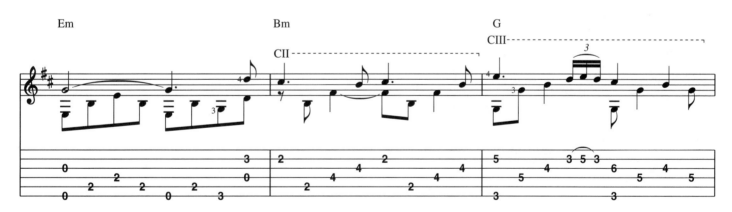

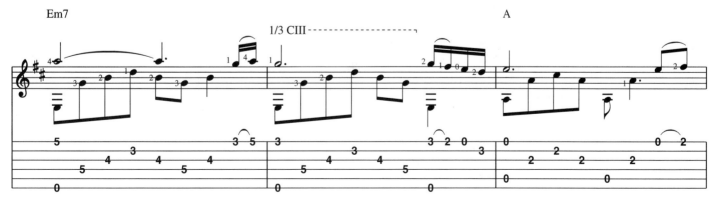

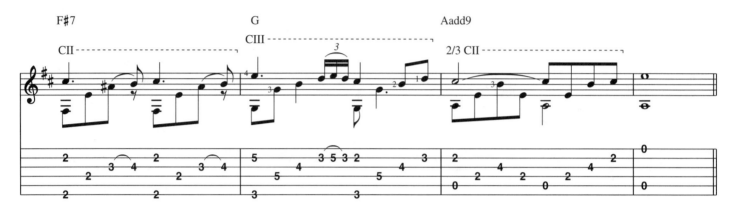

Stately, classical feeling

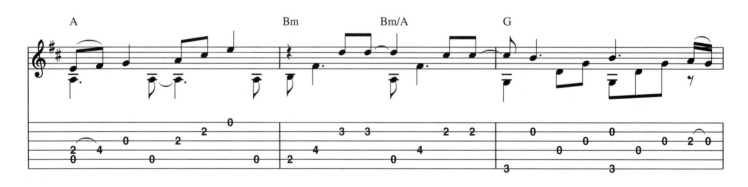

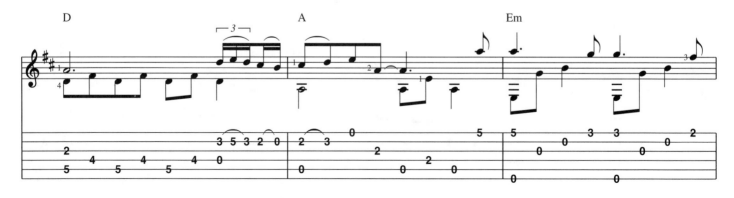

D.S. al Coda

⊕ Coda

Slowly, ethereal and sustained

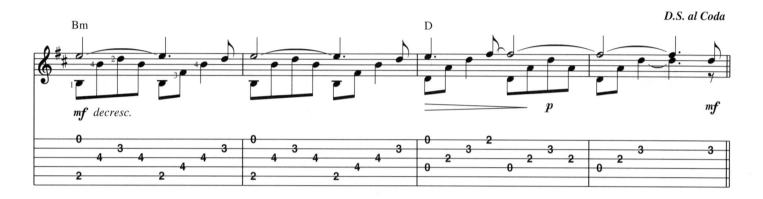

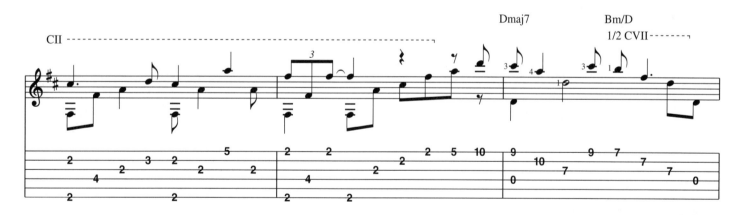

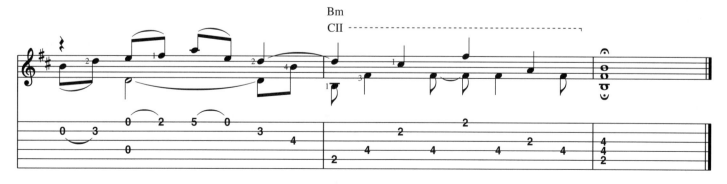

First Touch

Composed by Yanni

Drop D tuning:
(low to high) D–A–D–G–B–E

With graceful movement

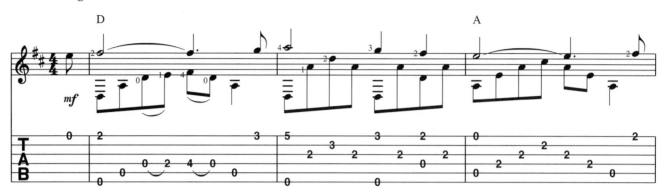

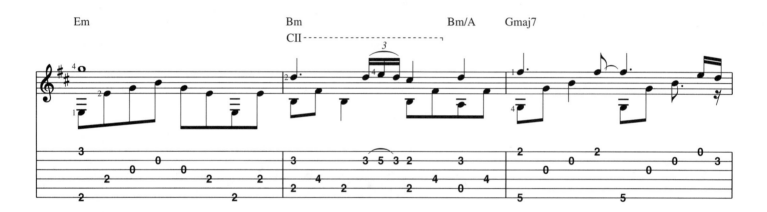

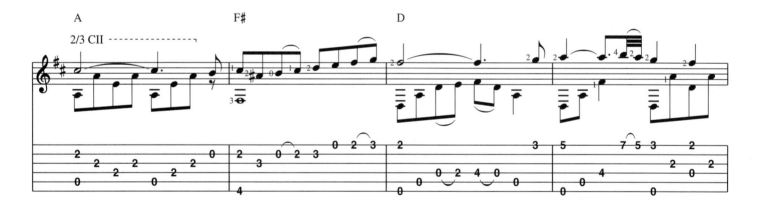

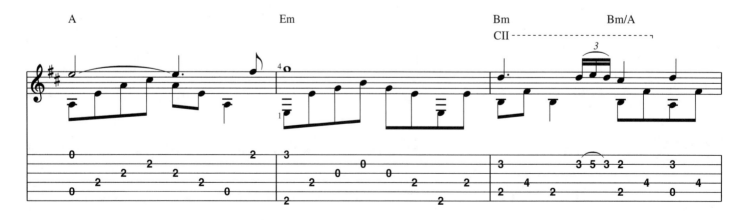

Delicately, ringing

With clarity, as in opening

Improvisationally

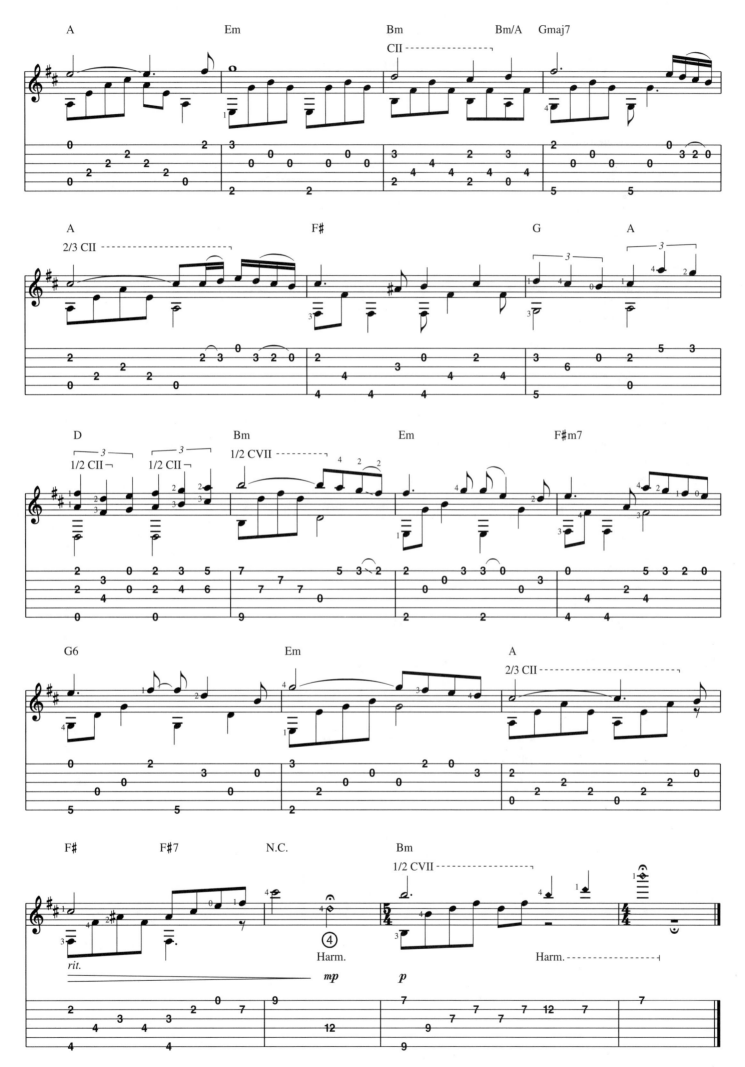

The Flame Within

Composed by Yanni

Moderately fast

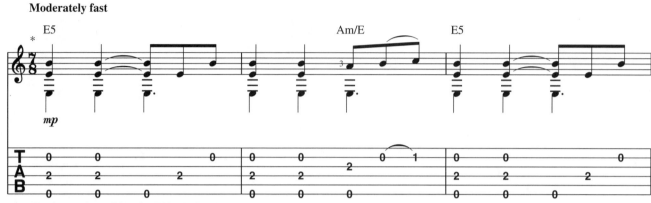

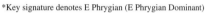

*Key signature denotes E Phrygian (E Phrygian Dominant)

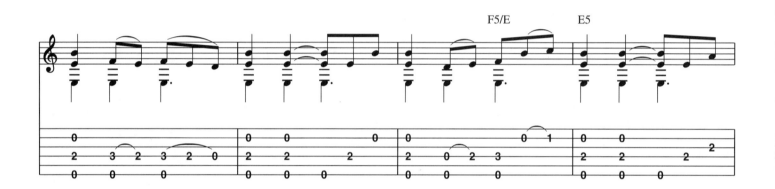

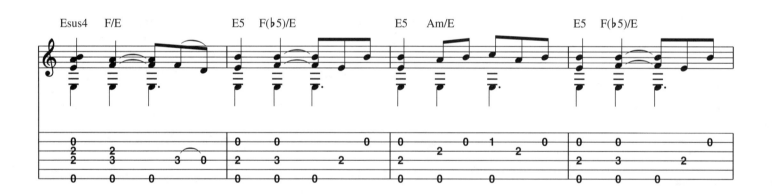

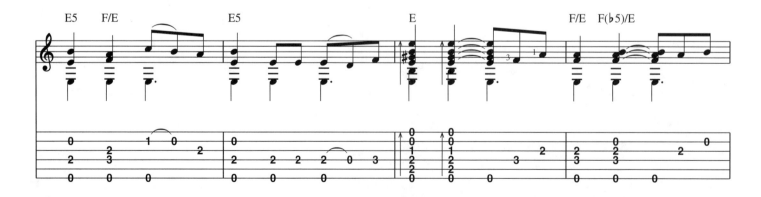

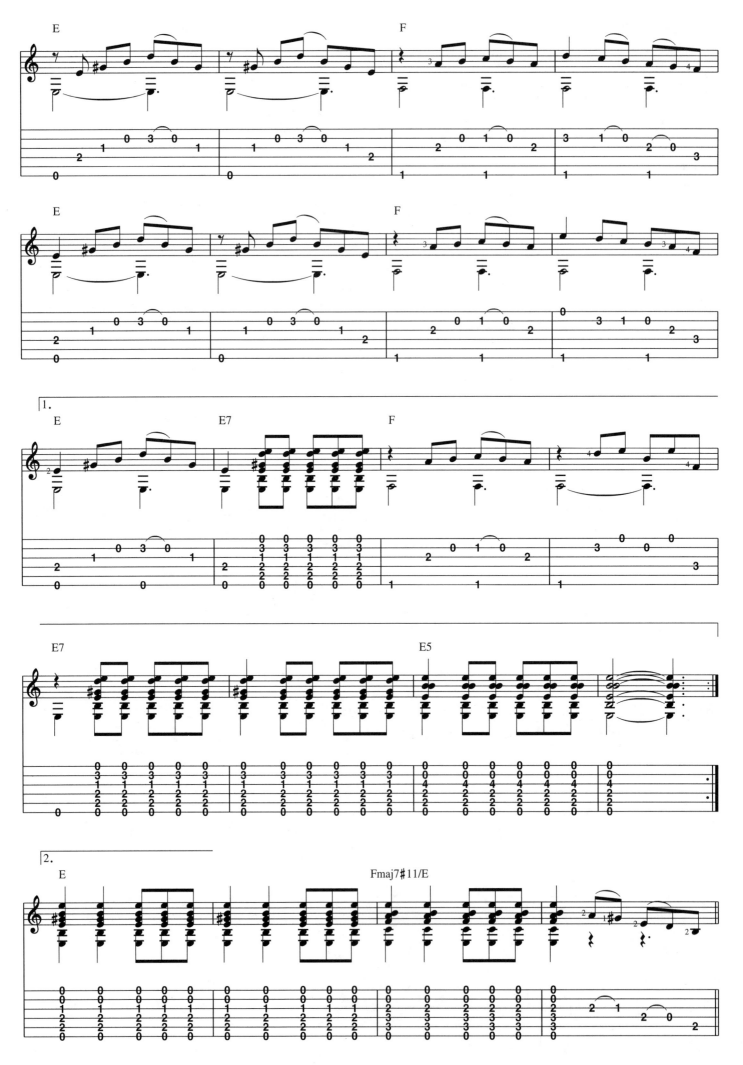

If I Could Tell You

Composed by Yanni

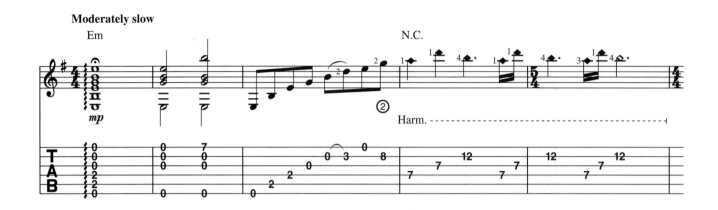

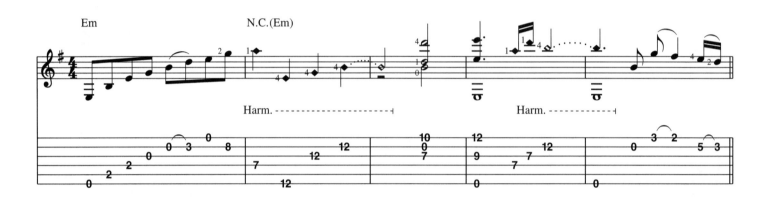

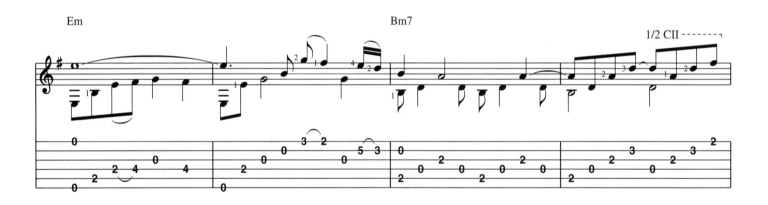

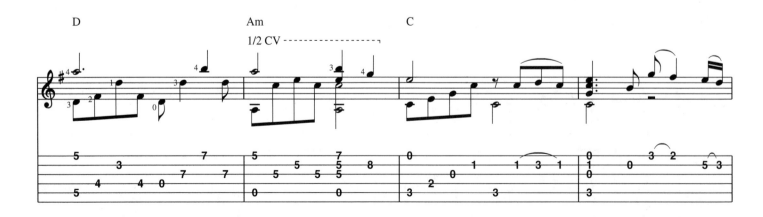

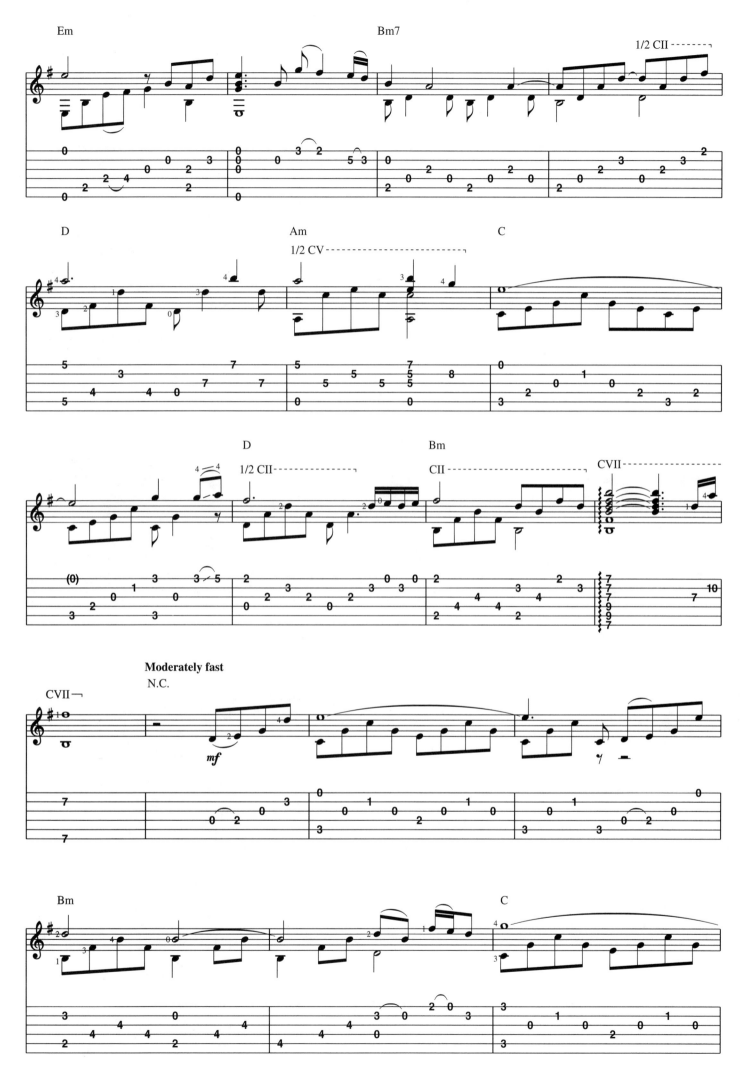

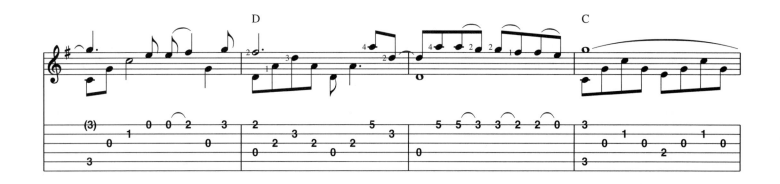

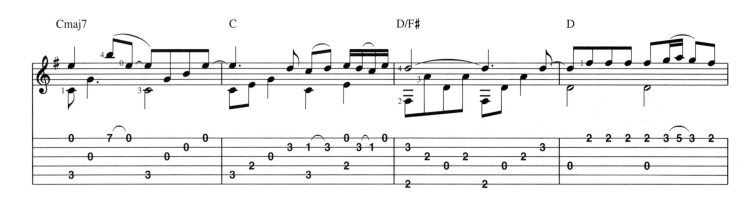

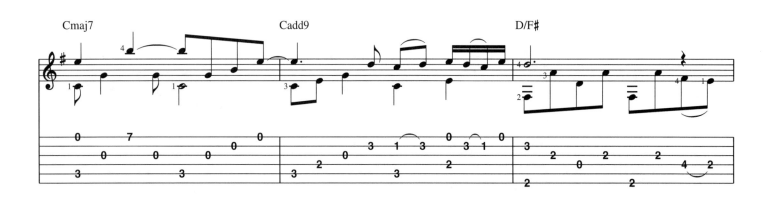

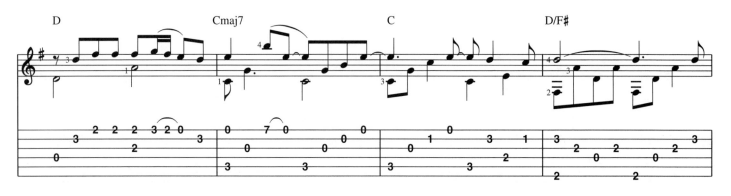

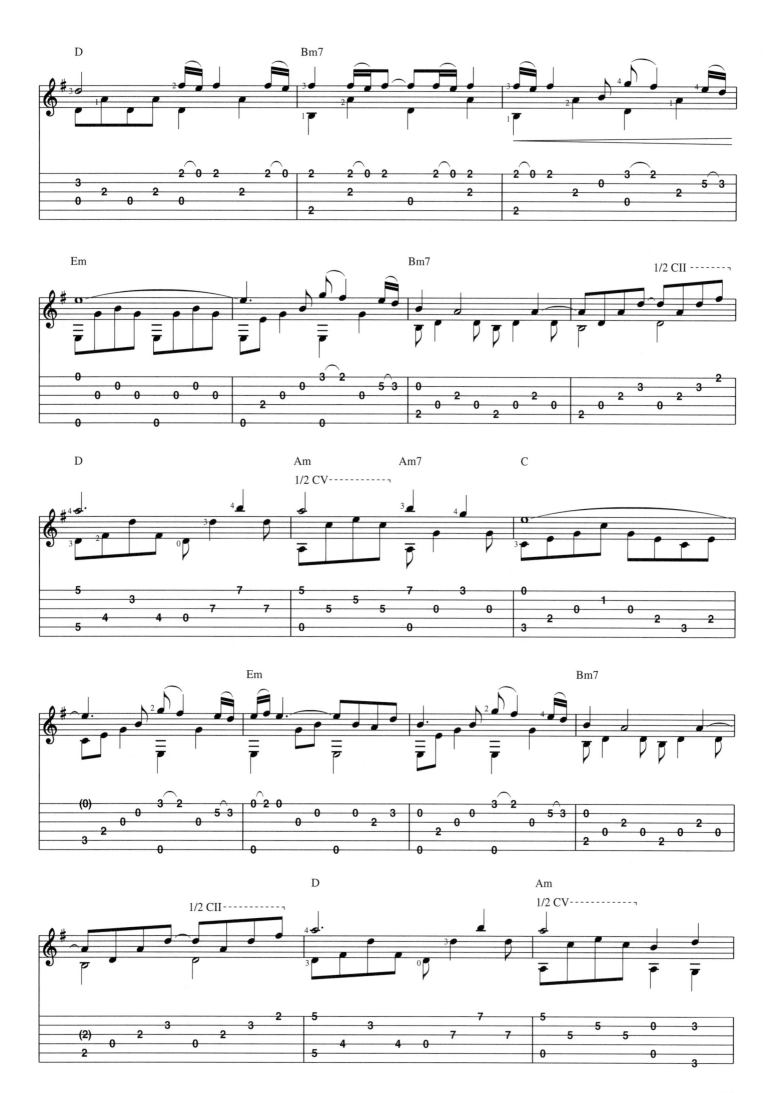

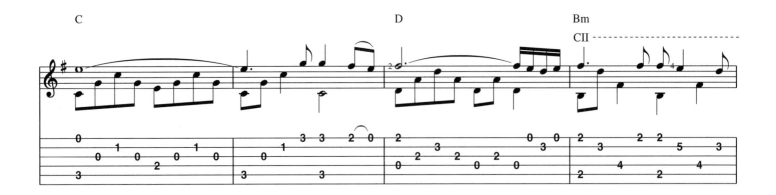

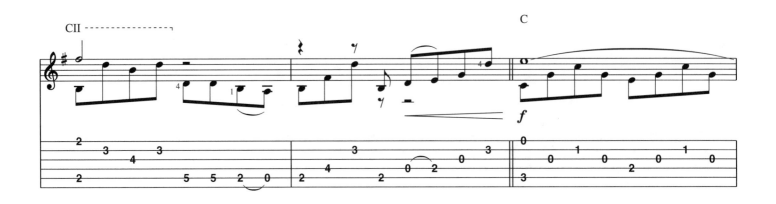

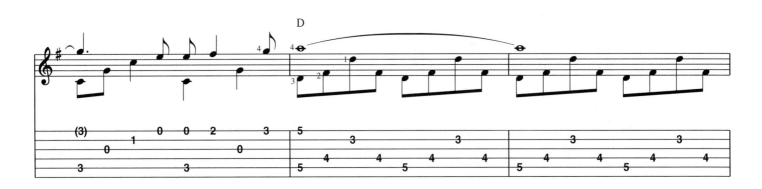

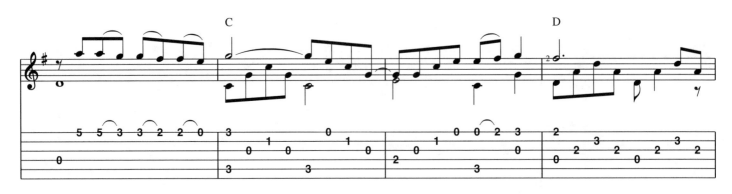

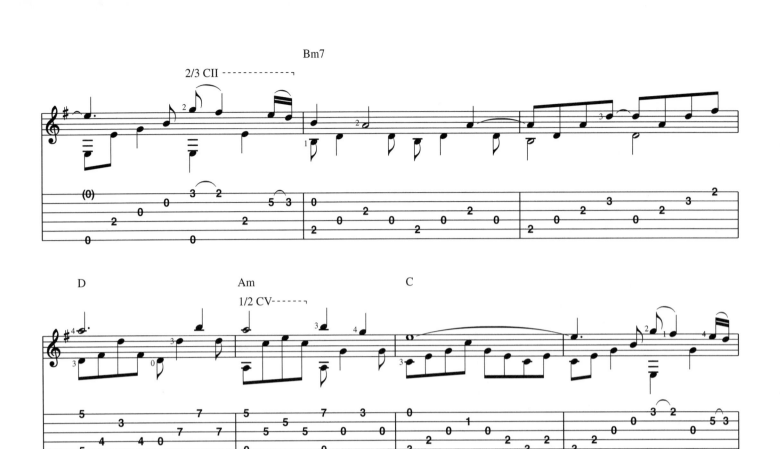

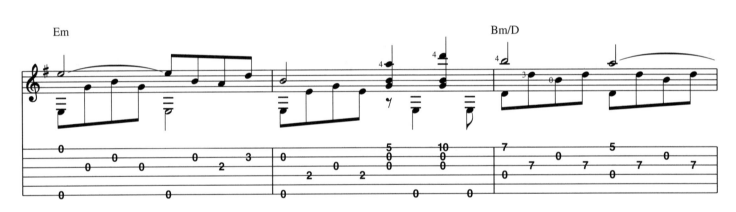

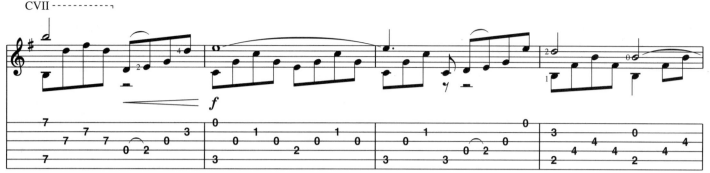
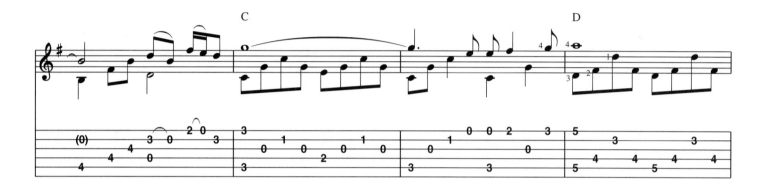

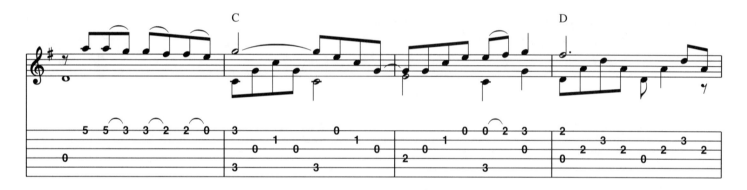
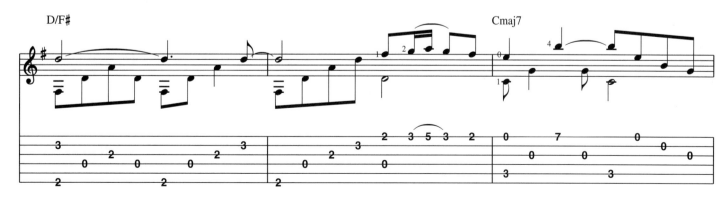

In Your Eyes

Composed by Yanni

Drop D tuning:
(low to high) D–A–D–G–B–E

Very slowly, freely

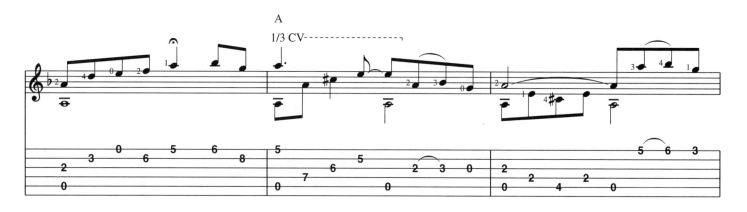

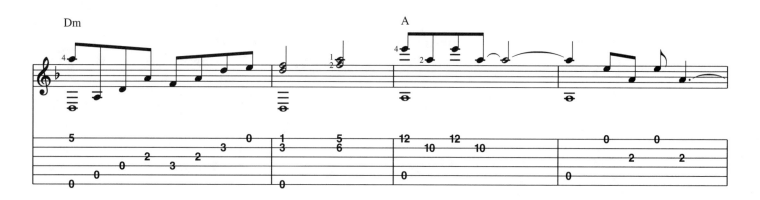

Moderately fast

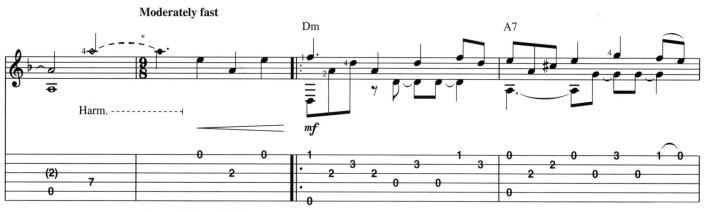

* measure division: 3+2+2+2

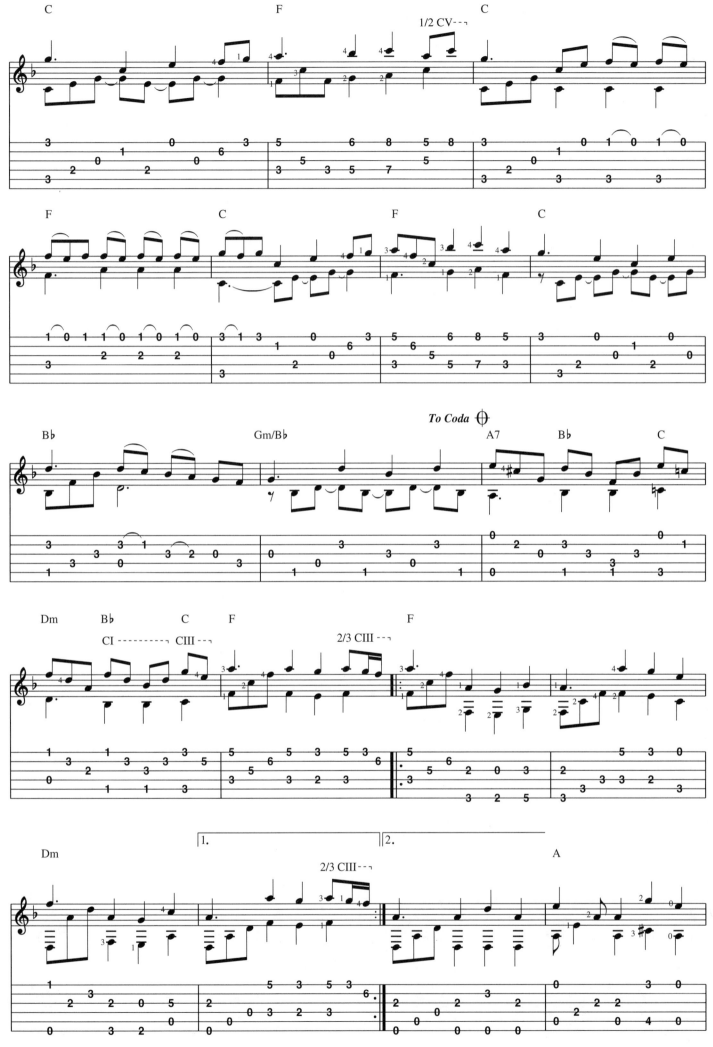

Nightingale

Composed by Yanni

* Strum as fast as sixteenth notes (w/ index finger).

True Nature

Composed by Yanni

Drop D tuning:
(low to high) D–A–D–G–B–E

Elegantly

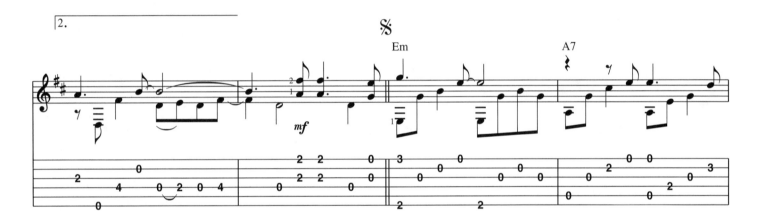

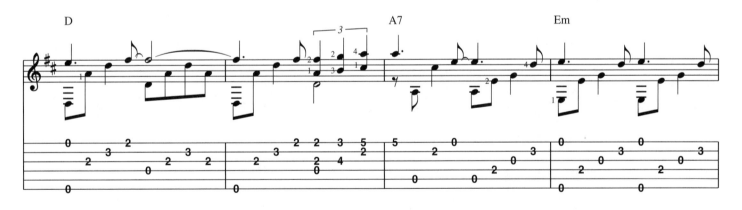

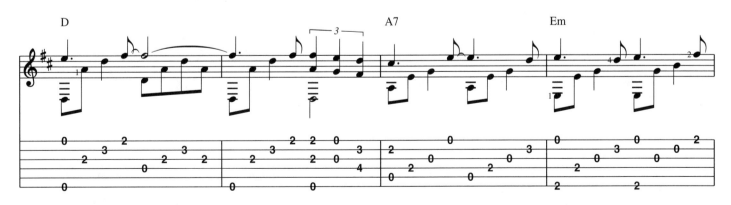

D.S. al Coda 1

Coda 1

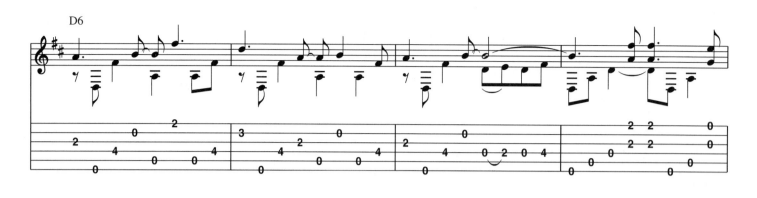

D.S.S. al Coda 2

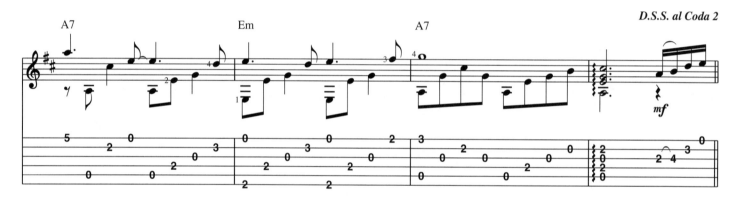

⊕ **Coda 2**

One Man's Dream

Composed by Yanni

Evenly, with inward intensity

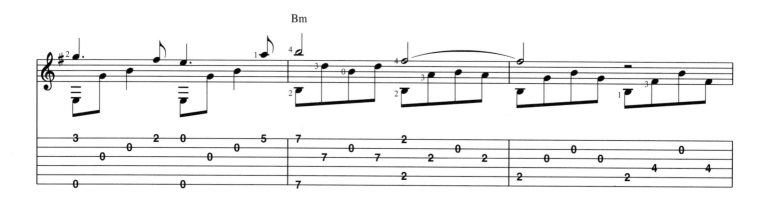

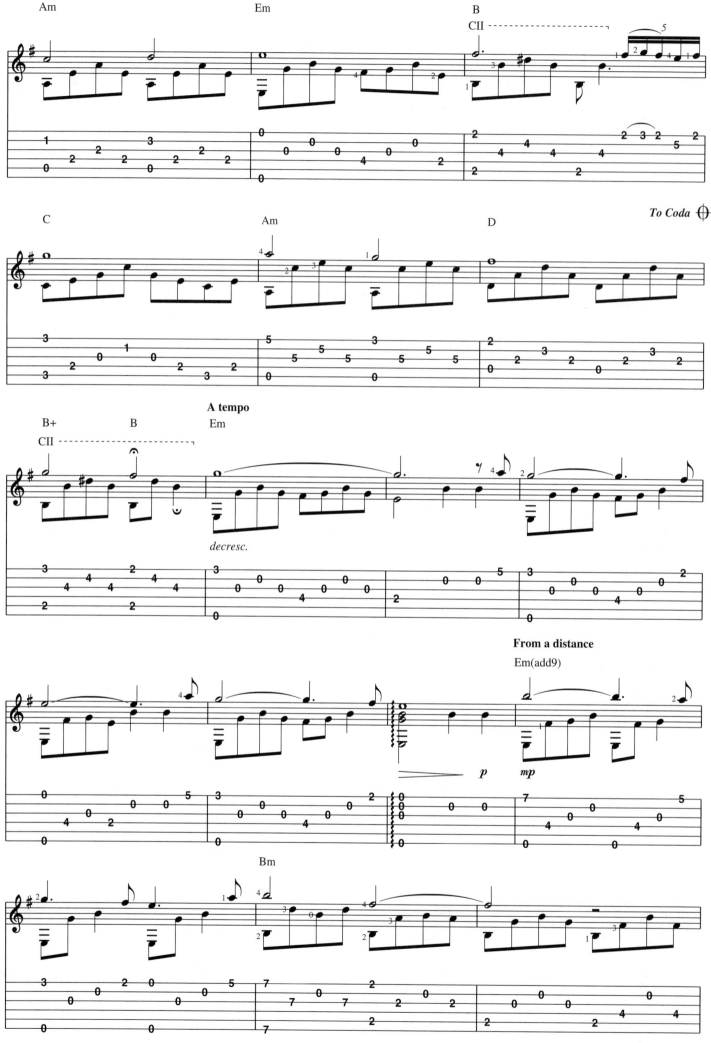

From a distance

Reflections of Passion

Composed by Yanni

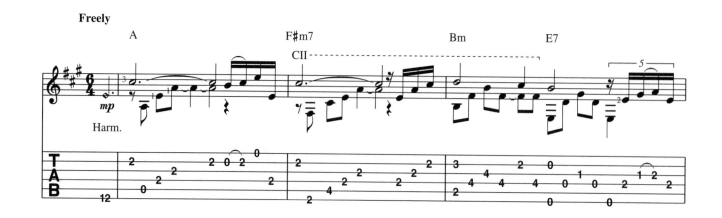

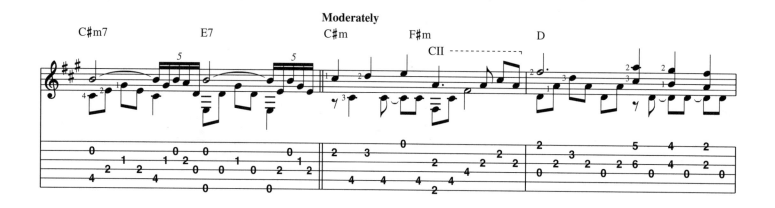

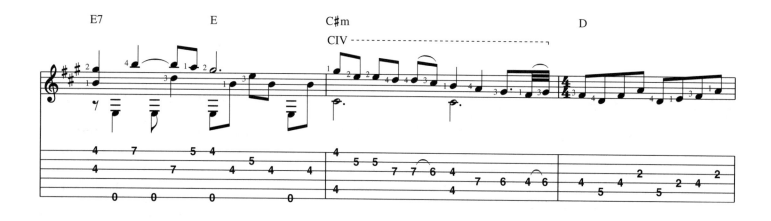

Gentle Waltz tempo

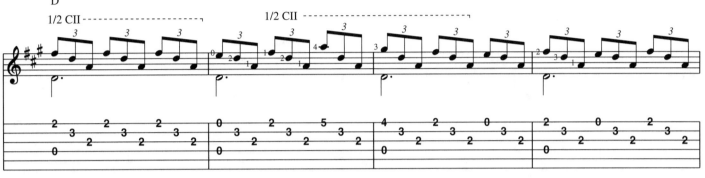

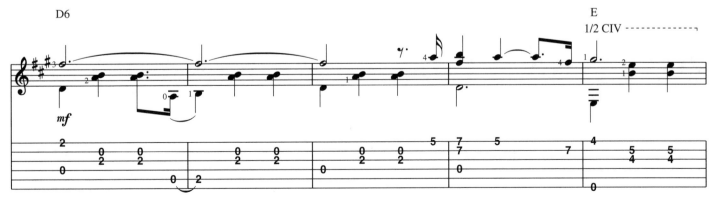

Secret Vows

Composed by Yanni

Drop D tuning:
(low to high) D–A–D–G–B–E

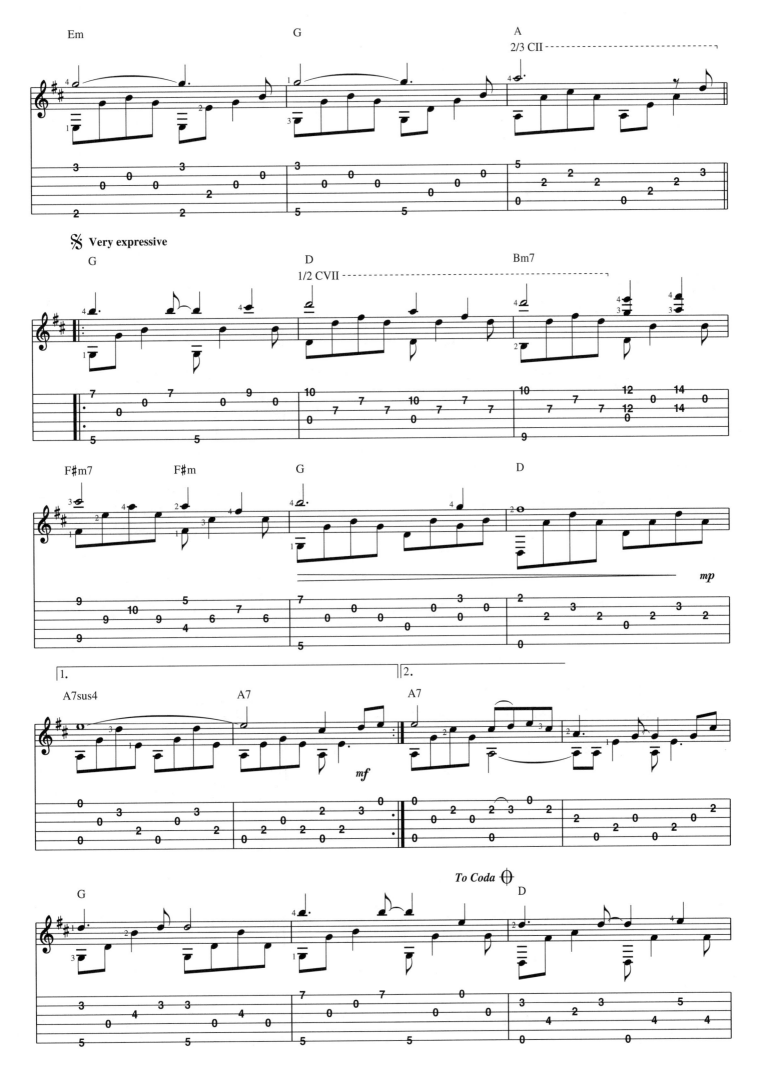

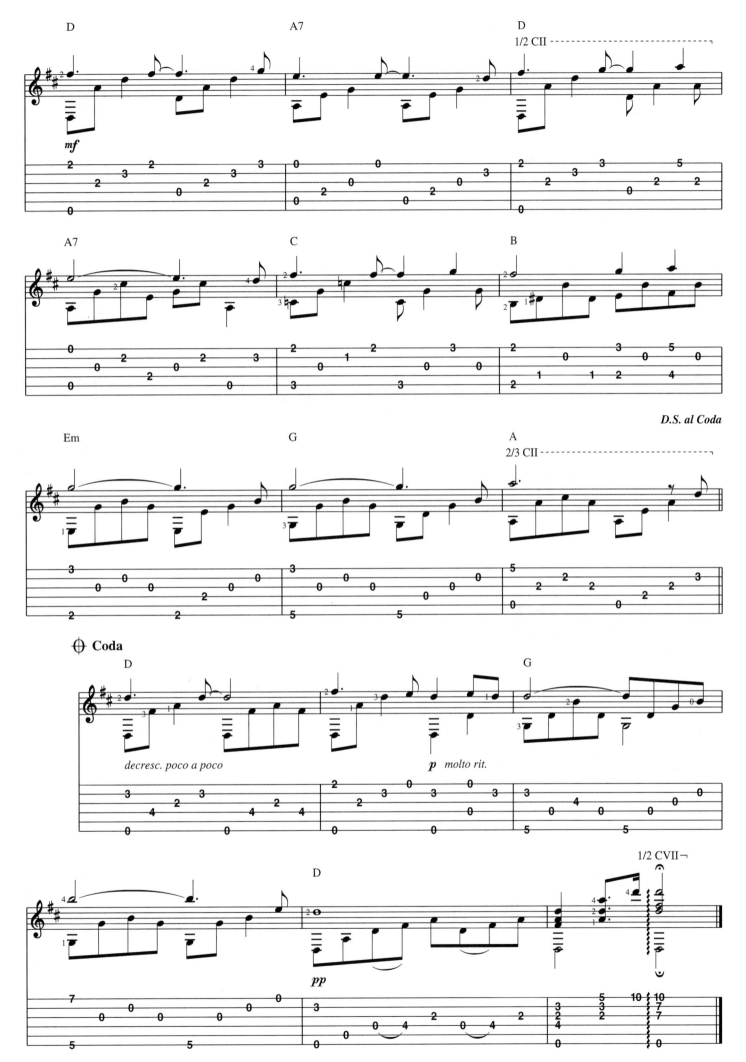

To Take..To Hold

Composed by Yanni

Drop D tuning:
(low to high) D–A–D–G–B–E

Evenly, peaceful

Stately

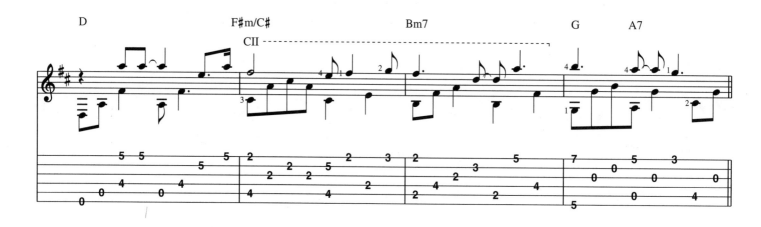

A Walk in the Rain

Composed by Yanni

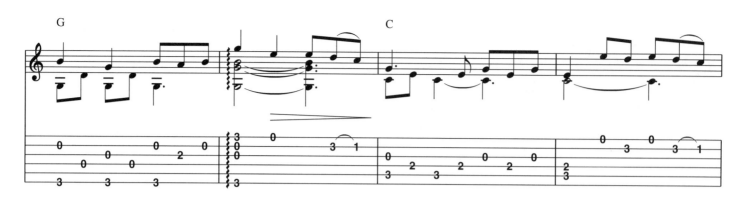

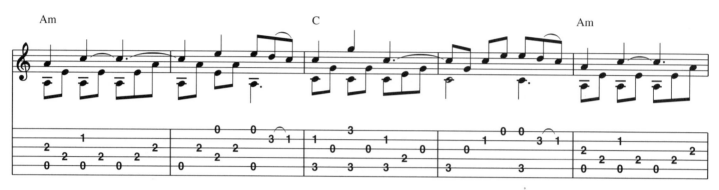

A Word in Private

Composed by Yanni

Relaxed but majestic

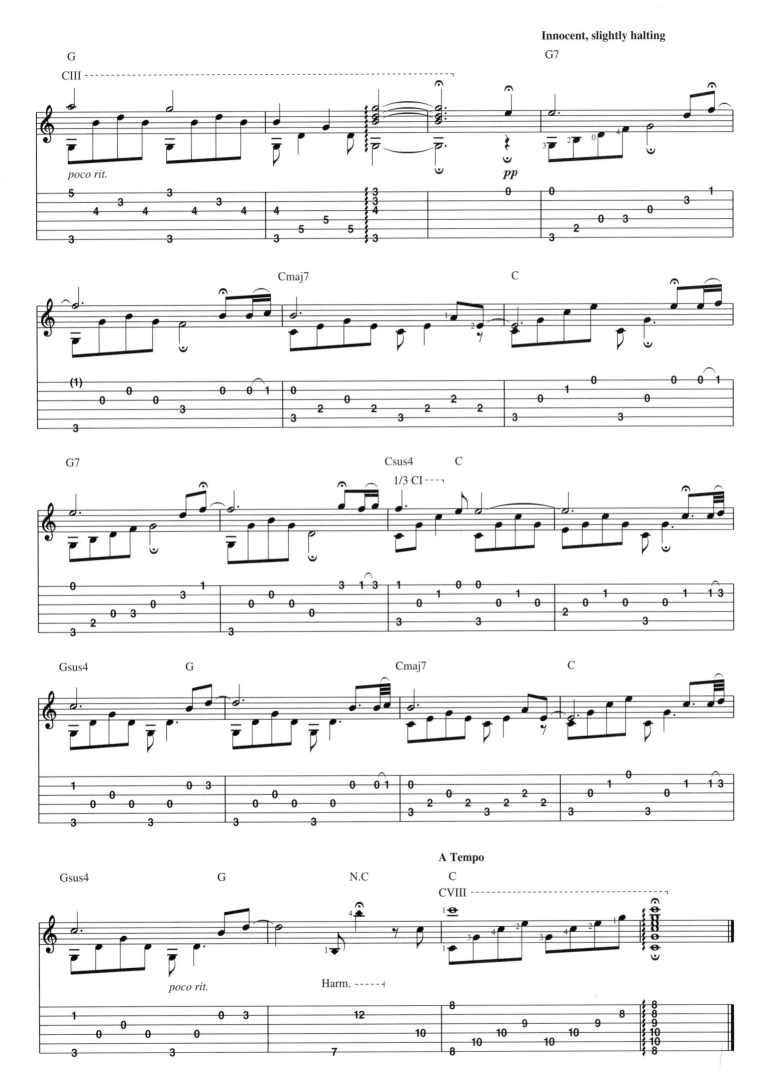

More Fingerstyle Favorites

from

HAL•LEONARD®

12 Wedding Songs
arranged for medium voice and fingerstyle guitar
The collection combines classical/traditional and popular selections. The guitar part is presented in both standard notation and tablature. Contents: Annie's Song • Ave Maria (Shubert) • The First Time I Saw Your Face • Here, There And Everywhere • I Swear • If • In My Life • Jesu, Joy Of Man's Desiring • Let It Be Me • Unchained Melody • When I Fall In Love • You Needed Me.
00740007 ....$12.95

American Folk Songs For Fingerstyle Guitar
25 songs, including: Amazing Grace • America The Beautiful • Home On The Range • I've Been Working On The Railroad • My Old Kentucky Home • When Johnny Comes Marching Home • and more.
00698981 ....$12.95

Broadway Ballads for Guitar
24 arrangements, including: All I Ask Of You • Bewitched • I Dreamed A Dream • Memory • My Funny Valentine • What I Did For Love • and more.

00698984 ....$10.95

Classic Blues for Voice and Fingerstyle Guitar
20 arrangements with guitar accompaniment and solos, including: Mercury Blues • Seventh Son • Little Red Rooster • Trouble In Mind • Nobody Knows You When You're Down And Out • and more.

00698992 ....$12.95

Contemporary Movie Songs For Solo Guitar
24 arrangements of silver screen gems, including: Endless Love • The John Dunbar Theme ("Dances With Wolves") • Theme From "Ordinary People" • Somewhere Out There • Unchained Melody • and more. Includes notes and tab.
00698982 ....$14.95

Disney Fingerstyle Guitar
14 fun favorites, including: Under The Sea • Beauty And The Beast • A Whole New World • Can You Feel The Love Tonight • and more.

00690009 ....$12.95

Gospel Favorites For Fingerstyle Guitar
25 classics, including: Amazing Grace • Because He Lives • El Shaddai • How Great Thou Art • The Old Rugged Cross • Rock Of Ages • Will The Cradle Be Unbroken • Wings Of A Dove • and more. Includes notes and tab.
00698991 ....$12.95

International Favorites
25 songs that span the globe, including: Au Clair de la Lune • The Blue Bells Of Scotland • La Cucaracha • Londonderry Air • Santa Lucia • and more.

00698996 ....$12.95

Mannheim Steamroller – Christmas For Fingerstyle Guitar
Enjoy these world-famous Christmas arrangements from the best-selling Mannheim Steamroller albums. 10 pieces, including: Carol Of The Birds • The Holly And The Ivy • I Saw Three Ships • Wassail, Wassail • and more. Includes notes and tab.
00650042 ....$12.95

Fingerpicking Beatles
20 favorites, including: And I Love Her • Eleanor Rigby • Here Comes The Sun •Here, There And Everywhere • Hey Jude • Michelle • Norwegian Wood • While My Guitar Gently Weeps • Yesterday • and more.

00699404 ....$14.95

Eric Clapton Fingerstyle Guitar Collection
12 Clapton classics for fingerstyle guitar. Includes: Bell Bottom Blues • Cocaine • Layla • Nobody Knows You When You're Down And Out • Strange Brew • Tears In Heaven • Wonderful Tonight • and 5 more favorites.

00699411 ....$10.95

A Fingerstyle Guitar Christmas
29 great fingerstyle arrangements, including: Angels We Have Heard On High • Auld Lang Syne • The First Noel • Good King Wenceslas • The Holly And The Ivy • Jingle Bells • O Little Town Of Bethlehem • Up On The Housetop • What Child Is This? • and more.
00699038 ....$12.95

Billy Joel – The Fingerstyle Collection
15 of his most popular hits arranged for fingerstyle guitar, including: Honesty • Just The Way You Are • My Life • Piano Man • Uptown Girl • and more.

00699410 ....$12.95

Elton John – The Fingerstyle Collection
15 fingerstyle arrangements, including: Your Song • Daniel • Bennie And The Jets • Crocodile Rock • Don't Go Breaking My Heart • Candle In The Wind • and more. Includes notes and tab.

00699414 ....$14.95

TV Tunes For Guitar
23 fingerstyle arrangements of America's most memorable TV themes, including: The Addams Family • The Brady Bunch • Coach • Frasier • Happy Days • Hill Street Blues • I Love Lucy • Mister Ed • Northern Exposure • The Odd Couple • St. Elsewhere • and more.
00698985 ....$12.95

FOR MORE INFORMATION, SEE YOUR LOCAL MUSIC DEALER, OR WRITE TO:

HAL•LEONARD®
CORPORATION
7777 W. BLUEMOUND RD. P.O. BOX 13819 MILWAUKEE, WI 53213
HTTP://WWW.HALLEONARD.COM

Prices, contents, and availability subject to change without notice. Some products may not be available outside the U.S.A.

THE BOOK SERIES
FOR EASY GUITAR

THE BLUES BOOK
84 super blues tunes: All Blues • Baby Please Don't Go • Double Trouble • Fine and Mellow • Honest I Do • I'm Your Hoochie Coochie Man • Killing Floor • Love Struck Baby • Mean Old World • Milk Cow Blues • Muleskinner Blues • Pinetop's Blues • Route 66 • See See Rider • Statesboro Blues • Texas Flood • Trouble in Mind • Who Do You Love • more.
00702104 Easy Guitar $14.95

THE BROADWAY BOOK
93 unforgettable songs from 57 shows! Includes: Ain't Misbehavin' • Beauty and the Beast • Cabaret • Camelot • Don't Cry for Me Argentina • Edelweiss • Hello, Dolly! • I Could Write a Book • I Whistle a Happy Tune • Mame • My Favorite Things • Oklahoma! • One • People • September Song • Some Enchanted Evening • Tomorrow • Try to Remember • Where or When • more.
00702015 Easy Guitar $17.95

THE CLASSIC COUNTRY BOOK
101 country classics: Act Naturally • Cold, Cold Heart • Could I Have This Dance • Crazy • Daddy Sang Bass • D-I-V-O-R-C-E • El Paso • Folsom Prison Blues • The Gambler • Heartaches by the Number • I Fall to Pieces • I'm Not Lisa • King of the Road • Kiss an Angel Good Mornin' • Lucille • Mississippi Woman • Rocky Top • Sixteen Tons • Son-of-a-Preacher Man • When Two Worlds Collide • Will the Circle Be Unbroken • You Needed Me • more.
00702018 Easy Guitar $19.95

THE CLASSIC ROCK BOOK
89 huge hits: American Woman • Beast of Burden • Black Magic Woman • Born to Be Wild • Cocaine • Dust in the Wind • Fly like an Eagle • Free Bird • Gimme Three Steps • I Can See for Miles • Iron Man • Lola • Magic Carpet Ride • Nights in White Satin • Reelin' in the Years • Revolution • Roxanne • Sweet Home Alabama • Walk This Way • You Really Got Me • and more.
00698977 Easy Guitar $19.95

THE GOSPEL SONGS BOOK
A virtual bible of gospel songs arranged for easy guitar. Features: Amazing Grace • At Calvary • Blessed Assurance • Church in the Wildwood • He Touched Me • His Eye Is on the Sparrow • How Great Thou Art • I Love to Tell the Story • I Saw the Light • Just a Closer Walk with Thee • More Than Wonderful • The Old Rugged Cross • Rock of Ages • Shall We Gather at the River? • Sweet by and By • Turn Your Radio On • Will the Circle Be Unbroken • and more.
00702157 Easy Guitar $16.95

THE HYMN BOOK
An inspirational collection of 146 glorious hymns arranged for easy guitar. Includes: Abide with Me • Amazing Grace • At the Cross • Be Thou My Vision • Blessed Assurance • Come, Thou Fount of Every Blessing • Fairest Lord Jesus • Holy, Holy, Holy • Just a Closer Walk with Thee • Nearer, My God, to Thee • The Old Rugged Cross • Rock of Ages • more. Perfect for church services, sing-alongs, bible camps and more!
00702142 Easy Guitar $14.95

THE JAZZ STANDARDS BOOK
100 standard songs in easy guitar format (without tablature). Songs include: Ain't Misbehavin' • Always • Autumn in New York • Blue Skies • Come Rain or Come Shine • Fly Me to the Moon (In Other Words) • Georgia on My Mind • God Bless' the Child • I Didn't Know What Time It Was • I've Grown Accustomed to Her Face • In a Sentimental Mood • It Don't Mean a Thing (If It Ain't Got That Swing) • The Lady Is a Tramp • Misty • My Funny Valentine • Slightly Out of Tune (Desafinado) • Stella by Starlight • The Very Thought of You • and more.
00702164 Easy Guitar $14.95

THE LATIN BOOK
102 hot Latin tunes: Amapola • Amor Prohibido • Bésame Mucho • Brazil • Cherry Pink and Apple Blossom White • Cielito Lindo • Frenesí • Granada • Guantanamera • It's Impossible • Mambo No. 5 • Mañana • María Elena • Perfidia • Spanish Eyes • Tango of Roses • Tico Tico • Vaya Con Dios • more.
00702151 Easy Guitar $16.95

THE LOVE SONGS BOOK
100 top love songs: Always • Body and Soul • Cheek to Cheek • Cherish • Don't Know Much • Emotions • Endless Love • Feelings • Fly Me to the Moon • For All We Know • How Deep Is Your Love • La Vie En Rose • Love Me Tender • Misty • My Romance • Something • You Were Meant for Me • Your Song • more.
00702064 Easy Guitar $16.95

THE NEW COUNTRY HITS BOOK
100 hits by today's top artists! Includes: Achy Breaky Heart • Ain't Going Down ('Til the Sun Comes Up) • Blame It on Your Heart • Boot Scootin' Boogie • Chattahoochee • Down at the Twist and Shout • Friends in Low Places • Honky Tonk Attitude • Neon Moon • Somewhere in My Broken Heart • Small Town Saturday Night • T-R-O-U-B-L-E • The Whiskey Ain't Workin' • more.
00702017 Easy Guitar $19.95

THE R&B BOOK
Easy arrangements of 89 great hits: ABC • Baby I Need Your Lovin' • Baby Love • Ben • Cloud Nine • Dancing in the Street • Easy • Emotion • Exhale (Shoop Shoop) • I Heard It Through the Grapevine • I'll Be There • I'm So Excited • Man in the Mirror • My Girl • Ooo Baby Baby • Please Mr. Postman • Sexual Healing • Stand by Me • This Masquerade • Three Times a Lady • What's Going On • more.
0702058 Easy Guitar $16.95

THE ROCK CLASSICS BOOK
89 rock favorites: Back in the Saddle • Bennie and the Jets • Day Tripper • Evil Ways • For Your Love • Free Ride • Hey Joe • Juke Box Hero • Killer Queen • Low Rider • Oh, Pretty Woman • Pride and Joy • Ramblin' Man • Rhiannon • Smoke on the Water • Young Americans • more.
00702055 Easy Guitar $16.95

THE WEDDING SONGS BOOK
This collection contains easy arrangements (without tab) for 94 songs of love and devotion appropriate for performance at weddings. Includes: Always • Endless Love • Grow Old with Me • I Will Be Here • Just the Way You Are • Longer • My Romance • Ode to Joy • This Very Day • Valentine • Wedding March • When You Say Nothing at All • A Whole New World • and many more!
00702167 Easy Guitar $16.95

FOR MORE INFORMATION, SEE YOUR LOCAL MUSIC DEALER, OR WRITE TO:

HAL•LEONARD®
CORPORATION
7777 W. BLUEMOUND RD. P.O. BOX 13819 MILWAUKEE, WI 53213

Prices, contents, and availablity subject to change without notice.

Visit Hal Leonard online at
www.halleonard.com